WITH THANKS

There are so many ways those around us make a difference for the better. Every day, their expressions of kindness and care make our lives brighter and our concerns lighter.

From a simple smile to a selfless offer of help, there are people who add incredible amounts of goodness to the world. And their support sparks a sense of appreciation in us that's difficult to measure.

When so much is given, sometimes all we can do is simply recognize how extraordinary these people really are and admire their dedication, with deepest thanks.

...the world needs hundreds of thousands more people like you.

EVETTE CARTER

*You are not only
good yourself,
but the cause of
goodness in others.*

SOCRATES

Too often we underestimate the power of... a smile, a kind word, a listening ear, an honest compliment, or the smallest act of caring...

LEO BUSCAGLIA

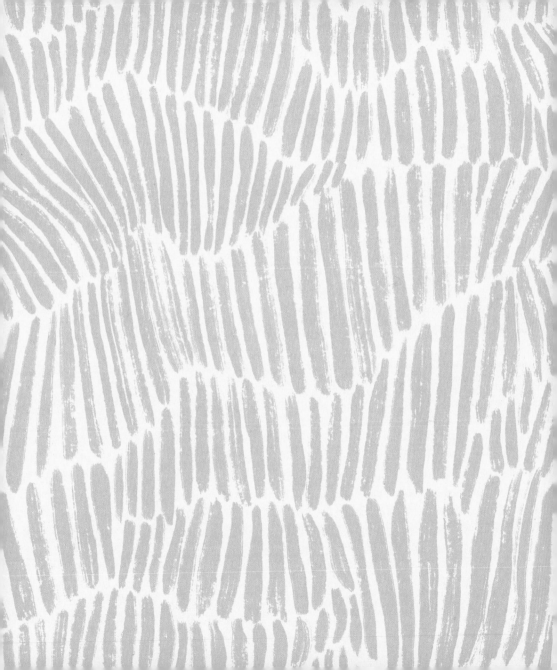

*It is wonderful
what one ray of
sunshine can do...*

FYODOR DOSTOYEVSKY

...YOU BRING
HAPPINESS
TO EVERYONE
YOU TOUCH...

Auriane Desombre

There can be no greater gift than that of giving one's time and energy to help others...

NELSON MANDELA

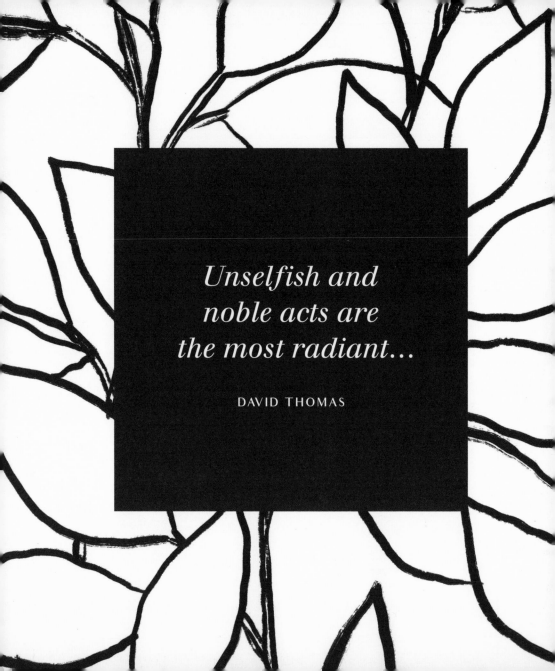

*Unselfish and
noble acts are
the most radiant...*

DAVID THOMAS

*Some people
make the world
more special just
by being in it.*

KELLY ANN ROTHAUS

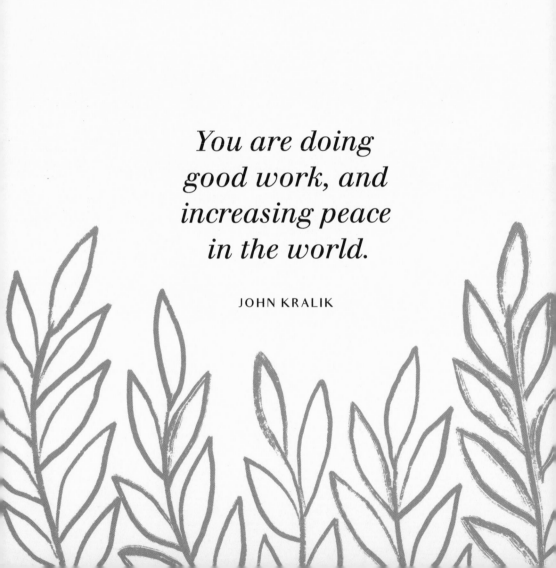

You are doing good work, and increasing peace in the world.

JOHN KRALIK

...HUMBLE,
HEARTY,
AND SINCERE
THANKS...

Mark Twain

The best people
in life make those
around them better.

BRIEN BOUYEA

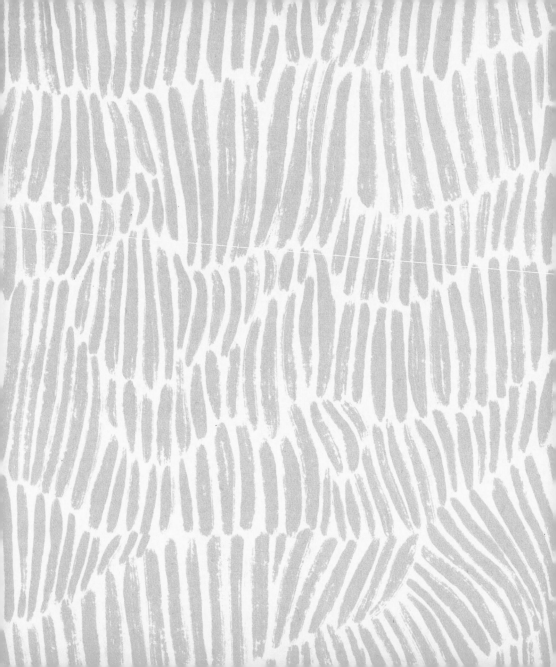

*Let's celebrate
everyone who is
planting and growing
seeds of goodness
into orchards that
nourish us all.*

FRAN I. HAMILTON

Each smallest act of kindness reverberates across great distances and spans of time... Because kindness is passed on and grows each time it's passed...

DEAN KOONTZ

...compassionate thought is the most precious thing there is.

DALAI LAMA

YOUR HELP WAS TREMENDOUS, NECESSARY, AND MUCH APPRECIATED.

Lisa Borne Graves

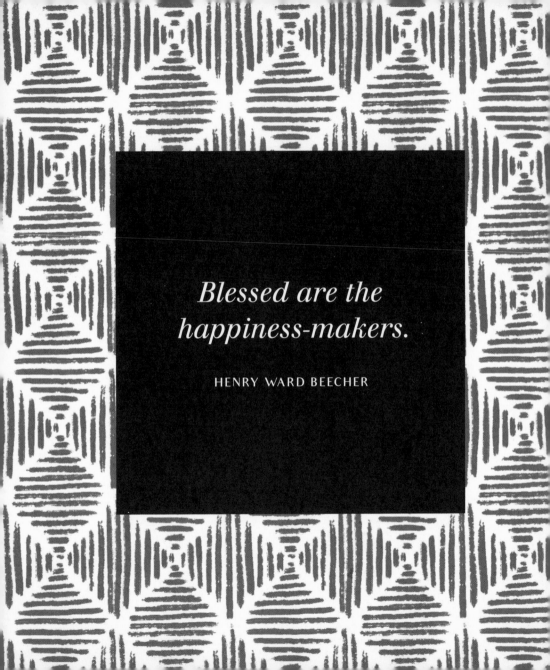

Blessed are the happiness-makers.

HENRY WARD BEECHER

A good deed is never lost.

SAINT BASIL THE GREAT

...THIS
KINDNESS
MERITS
THANKS.

William Shakespeare

At times our own light goes out and is rekindled by a spark from another person. Each of us has cause to think with deep gratitude of those who have lighted the flame within us.

ALBERT SCHWEITZER

THERE IS
NO EQUAL
TO YOU...

Bhagavad Gita

*...just a thank you for
being on this Earth...*

FRANZ KAFKA

The work of your heart,
the work of taking time,
to listen, to help, is also your
gift to the whole of the world.

JACK KORNFIELD

*It's the little things we do
and say, that mean so much
as we go our way.*

WILLA HOEY

MANY THANKS
FOR YOUR
KIND CARE...

Jane Austen

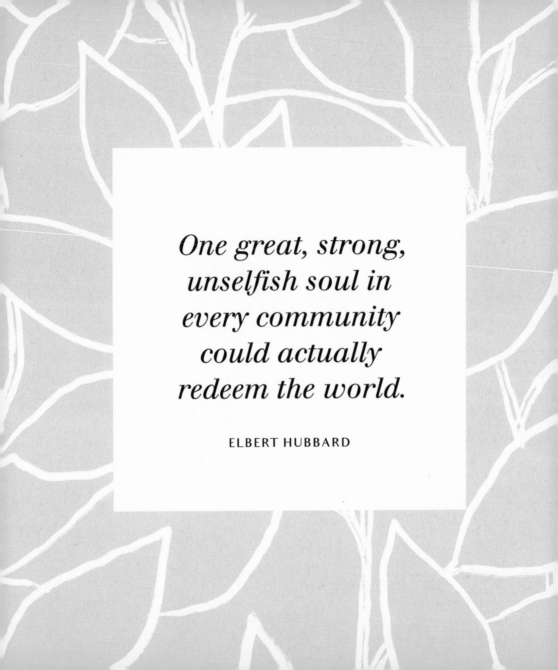

*One great, strong,
unselfish soul in
every community
could actually
redeem the world.*

ELBERT HUBBARD

HOW BEAUTIFUL A DAY CAN BE WHEN KINDNESS TOUCHES IT!

George Elliston

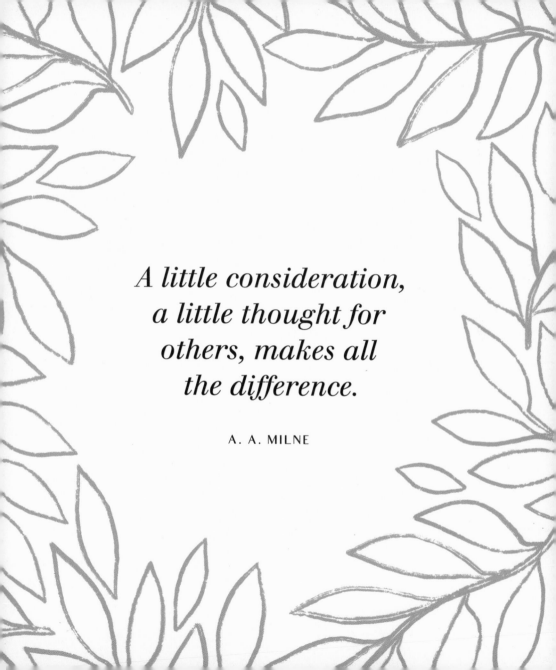

*A little consideration,
a little thought for
others, makes all
the difference.*

A. A. MILNE

*The simple act of
caring is heroic.*

EDWARD ALBERT

*Giving connects two people,
the giver and the receiver,
and this connects us all to
a new sense of belonging.*

DEEPAK CHOPRA

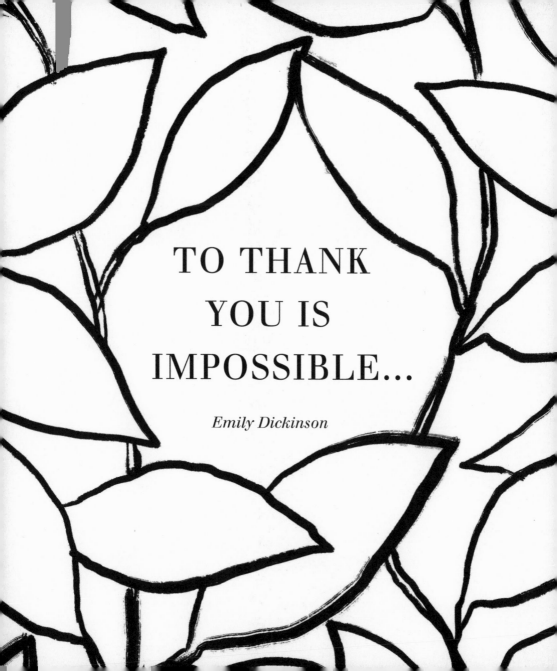

TO THANK
YOU IS
IMPOSSIBLE...

Emily Dickinson

There are those whose lives affect all others around them. Quietly touching one heart, who in turn, touches another. Reaching out to ends further than they would ever know.

WILLIAM BRADFIELD

*Caring is
the greatest thing,
caring matters most.*

FRIEDRICH VON HÜGEL